The Shapes We Make With Our Bodies

The Shapes We Make With Our Bodies

Published by Plays Inverse Press
New York, NY
www.playsinverse.com

ISBN 13: 978-0-9914183-3-6

First Printing: November 2015
Cover design by Adriana Lafarga
Page design by Tyler Crumrine
Printed in the U.S.A.

PLAYS INVERSE

The Shapes We Make With Our Bodies

MEG WHITEFORD

Plays Inverse Press
New York, NY
2015

To ghosts who stay close and voices that don't.

ACT I, SCENE I: WARM UP

This should be performed as an immersive play. Set at a real pool. But all the elements should be slightly elevated. The filter a bit too loud, the water a bit too blue, the weather just a bit too perfect.

ACT I, SCENE II: A THERAPEUTIC RELATIONSHIP

Well, we probably can't safely be in a real cavern so maybe a cavernous space so that all the voices echo and reverb. Like a church! Yeah, a church.

ACT I, SCENE III

This should be easy, lying outside. It should be on a hill. That seems like the most comfortable way to lie down and look up.

The women should build themselves into a frenzy. Tearing hair, gnashing teeth, clawing the ground, picking up their skirts and dancing in circles. In fact, there should be a ton of dancing throughout the entire play. As though the characters can't stop moving their bodies. All the while saying their lines inaudibly, increasing in volume and blurring over one another, cutting each other off. Let's hear what this sounds like and then we can always change it later.

ACT I, SCENE IV

The stage is now molten lava.

ACT II, SCENE I

These women just love lazing about so here we see

them at a spa. I think it'd be hard to produce at a real spa, so instead, let's cover the entire floor of whatever space we're in with jade and make it super hot and steamy. It'll smell clean and charcoal-like. You can come and lie down next to them, too, if you like.

ACT II, SCENE II

In a kitchen. Nothing special. I do want round-shaped cereal though.

ACT II, SCENE III

This should be a dark and secretive space. You have to brush past vines to find a door to a magical witchy room. The smell of incense should be overwhelming. Let's burn a ton of sage during this scene.

INTERLUDE: A HOCUS INTERROGATION

Darkened stage. How will the rocks perform? They are puppets, my dears.

ACT III, SCENE I: HONEY'S LAMENT, OR, THE BRIDGE ACROSS THE MOHAWK RIVER (OR, A TRIAL, OR, A FLASH-FORWARD)

Courtroom. But I feel like it should be a fake courtroom. Maybe set back on the lawn or in the church or at the pool. It should be aware of itself as a courtroom. In fact, maybe this whole thing should be fake.

ACT III, SCENE II: BANISHMENT

In the background, HONEY's silhouette moves along a cliff's edge.

HONEY, our central figure, a haunted woman, a woman running from her past and present; in her own world, very few direct addresses.

The MAENADS, three women, interchangeable, impish spies and instigators, love to play pretend, suckers for wordplay.

THERAPIST/VAMPIRA, curious, direct.

YOGA INSTRUCTOR/LION/OFFICER, scorned.

PRODUCTION NOTES

Instructions for dancing:

ACT I

THE SHAPES WE MAKE WITH OUR BODIES

It is the morning or early afternoon, I can't tell. The time seems to bleed together these days, doesn't it? Anyway. I digress. It is a gorgeous, cloudless, 78º day. The low-level hum of the filter and intermittent bubbling from the Jacuzzi gets louder and louder over the course of the scene until it drowns out all the voices. The pool should be the color of Gatorade Glacier Freeze®. Everyone looks slightly haggard, tired, hungover, but relaxed, as though there was nothing their bodies wanted more than to sit half-reclined in plastic chairs, avoiding eye contact either through closed eyes or sunglasses, and delivering lines as though each breath was a boulder being pushed up a hill over and over and over again. Someone should break the silence by cannonballing into the pool.

It is clear something happened last night. It is clear sacrifices were made, flesh was ripped. There was too much wine and greasy food ordered at 3 am. Voices were raised a few decibels higher than usual. It is clear we have entered this scene after some sort of shift. No, tectonic plates haven't moved. But, there has been a rupture. We may never know the details but bear with me. Try to stay in the present. I hear that is important.

Three intimidating women and HONEY, our bride and central figure, enter the pool in spandex workout clothes in various neons in a single line. They all have rolled-up mats under their arms. In synchronicity, they unfurl their mats and stand facing the leader, a male YOGA INSTRUCTOR. The YOGA INSTRUCTOR turns his back to the audience. He raises his arms like a conductor.

Deep breath, holding the breath for much too long.

> YOGA INSTRUCTOR. Hello everybody! [*repeats "Hello everybody!" in decrescendos until he can't go any slower or deeper in voice*]

Everybody laughs in various tones. The YOGA INSTRUCTOR begins to lead them in harmonious laughter. Ha ha ha ha ha ha....

YOGA INSTRUCTOR. Okay ladies, enough of this. Let's get going. We'll start with our warm up, then we'll move to the cardio with some classic boot camp moves, and then the cool-down and stretch-out. Let's begin in first position, arms in fifth.

Leads everyone through a warm up aerobic routine. Heels touch, toes turned out, bodies lifted, arms in front of bodies like hugging a large rubber ball, arms to the side like an awkward hug.

YOGA INSTRUCTOR. [*in a calm self-help-y voice*] Whew! Nice, ladies! Stay with me! Think of your bodies as slinkys! Think about discerning between your lefts and your rights. Think about kneading bread; think about avoiding laser beams. We are all square roots! Everyone be wall-like, now be pin-like, now be as a bell opening and closing and pausing.

The four women act this out:

YOGA INSTRUCTOR. Open your palms all fingers latched, separate and turn your hands to face one another, and turn them slowly back until all your fingers are touching. Now your bent hand touches your flat left palm, facing up. Your right palm arcs and the fingertips touch your left palm. Flick your pointers away quickly. Open your palms on your chest, one below the other, and open them away from your body, and close them in, and open them out, and close them in, and open them out, and close them in, and open them out, and close them in...

His voice fades away.

Everyone walks to the pool and begins to descend into the water in the way that most people who have learned about fear descend into water—faces twisted like raisins, knees lifted just a little bit too high, like they are lifting their limbs out of thick mud, rather than cool, crisp liquid.

Eventually, they make it in, submerge and reemerge merged in an embrace. They twirl in that sea lion way. They blow their bubbles, they let water run down their hair, their necks arch backwards, eyes closed in blissful reverie. All of that.

YOGA INSTRUCTOR. [*clapping hands*] Girls! Stay with me! We're almost there! Demonstrate a shiver.

ALL WOMEN TOGETHER. Shoulders tense, wiggle forward, bones creak, chest wanes, neck convulses up and out. There is a quick flick, like a flirt, of shoulders.

SOMEONE. CRAMP!

Everyone gasps and stares but does not move.

YOGA INSTRUCTOR. [*breaking the much too long silence*] Okay girls! Last set. Describe a spasm.

MAENAD 1. It is a wrenched raisin curled into itself breached body bent knees taut to chest in the way of holding oneself like a lima bean.

YOGA INSTRUCTOR. And how about the 50 seconds before a sigh?

MAENAD 2. Your synapses snap.

MAENAD 3. Heat enters your calves.

MAENAD 1. Heat enters your kneecaps.

HONEY. Heat enters your belly.

MAENAD 1. Heat enters your torso.

MAENAD 2. Your chest balloons outward.

MAENAD 3. Your belly balloons outward.

MAENAD 1. Your ribs move vertically.

HONEY. [*aside*] Is that God-ward?

MAENAD 1. Your throat constricts.

MAENAD 2. The inner corners of your eyes widen.

MAENAD 3. Your cheeks harden.

MAENAD 1. Your belly hardens.

HONEY. A sharpness appears.

MAENAD 1. You think of worms.

MAENAD 2. You think of floods.

MAENAD 3. You think of mazes.

MAENAD 1. You hold on.

HONEY. Then you let go.

YOGA INSTRUCTOR. [*aside*] Nothingness.

MAENAD 1. Nausea sets in.

MAENAD 2. Fear returns.

MAENAD 3. You struggle to find your lungs.

MAENAD 1. But they were never there.

HONEY. You struggle to unbury your throat.

MAENAD 1. Pry it open with the jaws of life.

MAENAD 2. Down the esophagus, surgically, with all your strength.

MAENAD 3. Eyes squinted.

MAENAD 1. Teeth gritted.

HONEY. You manage a grunt.

MAENAD 1. Your arm muscles tense.

MAENAD 2. You can't quite break through.

HONEY. So you break down.

MAENAD 3. Pour acid on your soft mouth flesh.

MAENAD 1. Tickle and sway, move that hot liquid around.

MAENAD 2. With a muscular tongue.

MAENAD 3. A light will appear.

YOGA INSTRUCTOR. It will pull the hole open wider.

HONEY. [*aside*] Wholer?

MAENAD 1. More light comes out of your mouth.

MAENAD 2. Your belly softens.

MAENAD 3. Your kneecaps soften.

MAENAD 1. Your calves soften.

MAENAD 2. Everything softens.

HONEY sneaks away.

MAENAD 1. There is a rumble in your vocal cords.

MAENAD 2. All the light in the world bursts through.

MAENAD 3. Your lips part.

MAENAD 1. Your eyes stumble.

ALL. A relief.

All sigh.

Cavernous stage. Enter the MAENADS, attached to one another, including HONEY, at the waist, arms wrapped around each other with binoculars set to her eyes. It's just like when you were young and you would step on your father's feet and he would pick you up with his steps. Your legs: mechanical; your father: Frankenstein's monster.

There is music playing with no coherent melody, strobing lights, an overwhelming smell of Palo Santo incense.

Shapes brightly colored blue, green, and pink that contrast with the deep hues of the backdrop—indigo, beetroot, ultramarine, fizz and pop and tumble into this cavern. Great towers and mountains burst upward, violently and majestically. Sparks like matches striking fill the indigo space with light. Citadels and walls arrange themselves horizontally, brick by brick, shape by shape. There are no ceilings, only walls, winding through the abyss in end-less and ever-ending corridors.

Hundreds of half-full water glasses cover the stage. Some are filled with soda.

MAENAD 1. It's dark in here.

MAENAD 2. Not dark, but an indigo darkness blanket.

MAENAD 3. I will sit patiently in the middle of the bottom of this pit, if you could call it that—there is no language here for landforms.

MAENAD 1. I am thinking of nothing.

MAENAD 2. I must put the shapes into ordered structures.

MAENAD 3. Monuments to the dead,

MAENAD 1. churches,

MAENAD 2. huts,

MAENAD 3. aqueducts,

MAENAD 1. bathhouses,

MAENAD 2. roads,

MAENAD 3. paths,

MAENAD 1. stairs,

MAENAD 2. halls,

MAENAD 3. meeting houses.

HONEY. The surge of the filling cavern reaches my ears. Just when I think I will drown (even though I never do), the eyes open up and all the shapes fly out. I am left alone, to wait again for the second blink.

MAENAD 1. I am a racing mind.

MAENAD 2. I am the gnawing feeling.

MAENAD 3. I am your caffeine addiction.

MAENAD 1. I am a headache and a heartache and a tummy ache and the uplift, the skipped beat, the elevation.

MAENAD 2. I am behind-the-eye hallucinations.

MAENAD 3. I am that thing caught in your throat.

MAENAD 1. That feeling in the pit of your stomach, warning you, or, urging you.

MAENAD 2. When your eyes are closed I am very eloquent.

MAENAD 3. I have no gut feelings, my words are never taken from me.

HONEY. [*stopping short*] What's that? I hear a dirge echoing through reeds.

MAENAD 1. I can see a somber party of eight blind men carrying a limp, wiry corpse toward the forest in the distance. The procession stops at a clearing in the woods, their lament rising to the canopy. A woman, eyes closed, reveals herself through a head laid on a shoulder.

HONEY. [*horrified*] Stop, don't go on.

MAENAD 1. A man's stingray back reaches inward, flexing wing bones. Four feet arch in third position, legs spread in mantis pose. Two bodies, crepuscular, are cleaving desperately to one another, as though tethering themselves with tight grasps only.

HONEY. [*disbelief*] It can't be.

MAENAD 2. Still, still body, face up.

HONEY. I smell blood and cum mixed with mint.

MAENAD 3. The woman shoves a handful of violets

into her mouth. She macerates the flowers into a paste and applies this salve to her lover's eye.

HONEY. [*hands to face*] I'm sorry.

MAENAD 1. Then, as though he was weightless, and perhaps he is, the woman scoops her arms under his and carries him away, wailing.

HONEY walks over in shock to the side of the stage where—and how did we not notice this before—there is a large velvet chair, a fainting sofa, and a floor lamp. A dragon dressed as a woman dressed as a THERAPIST sits in the chair. She puts on spectacles, crosses her legs at the hip, takes out a notebook, and turns on the floor lamp. All other lights go out.

HONEY lies down on her back on the fainting sofa and stares at the ceiling.

The MAENADS should writhe on the floor while offering their various interjections.

THERAPIST. What was that all about?

HONEY. Oh, it was just a feeling I had.

THERAPIST. What does that mean? An Assumption? A gut feeling? Your body existing in the mind's plane?

HONEY. No, it's an infection, I'm infected with language. How much language can one body contain?

THERAPIST. It must be released.

HONEY. But how does that work?

THERAPIST. First, there is an elevated feeling, a lift, and then a receding, an absorption back into yourself.

HONEY. The words are dribbling from my mouth forming caves of foreign languages in which I grasp around blindly for meaning. I can't speak fast enough to translate the feeling.

THERAPIST. So you're constipated with words?

HONEY. Very funny. No, I'm merely speechless.

THERAPIST. I wouldn't worry, I think it's just heat lightning, flashes of light punctuating the darkness, but never touching down. It could just be eyes that never adjust.

HONEY. You're probably right. Only the memory is allowed to rumble, and that feeling of being in a body disappears.

All the women swoon.

HONEY. [*groaning*] I feel like I'm going to ooze out through my eyeballs.

THERAPIST. We could all use a change of scenery.

HONEY. Maybe if I press my palms to my face, I can shove myself back inside. I feel dusty, my brain feels dusty.

THERAPIST. It won't work—the lines in your hands are carved too thick. The voids have become absolutely physical. Think of the carvings not as removals, but as insertions into space.

HONEY. [*to no one, really*] The truth is, I still really miss her.

THERAPIST. [*leans in, intrigued*] Tell me about this heartache.

HONEY. [*banging fist against her chest, and enacting the movements as she speaks them*] Baboom baboom baboom baboom. Closed fist knocks against chest, wrenched clenched fists over one another, just like twisting a towel, V fingers pull twist in, just like twisting a towel.

MAENAD 1. [*speaking up but still writhing, always writhing, maybe twitching*] What if you placed one end of a straw in your mouth and the other end in the hole in your heart and spent the rest of your life breathing into that makeshift lung?

MAENAD 2. [*still writhing like snakes*] It's curious how all lungs break in the same direction—up out down in closing and opening bodies.

(*Ditto.*)

MAENAD 3. Or, try sewing inlays into tiny pockets, as containers for your bones, your necklines, and the frogs in your throats.

HONEY. The edges of my body are the next closest things to elsewhere. Waiting to, or trying not to, leap out. Outside the edges are beginnings, searching for their middles and ends. Avoiding those other edges—The Choices. My words are left and fossilized in that self-made hole: the grave of a decision.

THERAPIST. [*takes off glasses, rubs bridge of nose*] What is the frame of your skin? Are you also made of chicken wire?

HONEY. Tent poles holding skin taut to ground tied too tightly, desperate to snap, to bend too far and fling upward, sending the skin flying into the sky, to quiver parachute-like slowly downward as we gaze upward mouths agape at the sight of the inside of the skin, inverted dragon fruit, inching its way back to earth, drifting at the will of the wind.

THERAPIST. [*takes out pocket watch and swings it back and forth in front of HONEY's eyes*] Tell me about the bones.

HONEY. [*falling into hypnosis*] The bones have snapped. Some long time ago they fused together at each lasting fracture with old gum. Worn tendons. Pile of bones on the ground, insides seeping out you couldn't say quickly—staining the earth ochre. Oozing goo spreading into the river of mud until you can't tell the intestines from the algae—they are all one massive globule—not quite liquid, a congealed solid. The resting blob on the earth with these broken and twisted bones, some are resting on top, some are protruding in and out, and there goes that parachute of skin dilly-dallying down, carried away, like a balloon on a highway.

THERAPIST. [*leans back, hands behind head, on the back two legs of her chair—satisfied pose*] Now we're talking.

MAENAD 1. [*picking up a glass of water and filling her mouth and speaking*] You know, you can measure the interior of your mouth by the volume of water you drink from your glass.

HONEY. [*snapping out of her hypnosis and turning to the MAENADS*] But I'm looking for someone with a beautiful mouth, containing nothing but echoes. My own throat is barren, the surfaces have been abraded by breath. Hear that? It's a tickle in my throat.

THERAPIST. [*grabbing HONEY's chin and turning her face back to hers*] Can you describe the noise?

HONEY. It was the sound of bursting; of boiling over pots on gas stoves; of ears popping further than the lobe; of no ears at all. It was the sound of discovery; all sounds reaching toward silence, then the silence.

Silence.

MAENAD 2. [*also filling her mouth with water*] Did you know that blood vessels can cry?

MAENAD 3. [*soda, burping*] You can soothe them with pleached honeyed tongues. Grafted words left uncured render language useless.

All three MAENADS roll on their backs and spit beverages up into the air while performing snow angels Busby Berkeley style. Burp.

HONEY. Do you mean I'm tongue-tied?

THERAPIST. [*enacting these words:*] I mean viper fingers thrust toward your mouth. I mean two fists, planetary, over and under pulling away from the rotation. I mean a tongue, that river of forgetting, extended. Mimicked. Mirrored. Imagine: words evaporating when spoken, river rock skipping, drunk on the flood-like spit frothing rabid from your limp muscle. I mean words congealed. Anyway, tell me about those seizures.

HONEY. As a child, I was afflicted with chronic tinnitus. My mother told me I was receiving radio transmissions from meteorites.

THERAPIST. What did that sound like?

HONEY. There were burst words and the noise of memory, there was coordinating between breathing (ahem) and voice (ha), and repeating sharp breaths.

Everyone repeats sharp breaths until they are all laughing. Burps.

THERAPIST. What a wild wave—like déjà vu! [*leaning in, hands table-top under chin, eyes so wide*] And then what?

HONEY. Tingly auras, funny turns, lips smacking, chewing, swallowing, blinks. Upwardly rotating eyes, rigorous shuddering, then evaporation.

THERAPIST. Very interesting! Describe a sigh.

HONEY. It is a tightening. Bones moving upward eyes perhaps widening then closing and remaining closed lingering behind eyelids. Belly extending. Throat constricting. A moment of sincere recognition of something that made you lose your breath. And then your chest moved up and you struggled for air. This is what it must feel like to be submerged.

THERAPIST. Would gills help?

HONEY. Sometimes finding the air is a relief. Other times it is a resignation. The truth is, I still really miss her.

THERAPIST. Hm, interesting, interesting! Here is what I would recommend:

Pay attention
to your limbs,
use your muscles.
Through motion,
a mere witnessing,
you can transcend forgetting.

Perform
the sedated dance
enshrouded by inverted voices,
echoes of a great chorus.

Take
strange awkward leaps,
bending, measuring
the counts
of the duration of holding.

Shadow box
at a glare.

Form constants
while you hallucinate—
honeycombs, webs, spirals.

Together, let's hover
on the edge
of infectious panic.

The THERAPIST turns off the light. Complete darkness for a very long time.

The three MAENADS—the same three women exercising at the pool—are lounging on their backs on a grassy hill in the now abandoned golf course staring at the sun, licking popsicles. FYI: They have all just dosed themselves with mushrooms.

I don't know what you see here but I see jewel toned lights cotton candy lush backdrops sparkling things satin things oozing from all corners things dangling bursting upward (stalagmites) and jutting downward (stalactites) I see interior lightning storms I see torrents I see tempests I see a river of Lethe running aquamarine perhaps it too is filled with crystals or perhaps that's confectioner's sugar I see dancing in concentric circles never-ending ripples inward and outward movements avoiding eye and body contact never-ending whirl pooling stirring the pot I see turkey leg meat juice frosting dripping on chins I see four tablespoons of butter talking with mouths full of spit and sweat and yellowed eyes glaring I see children screaming lines over the torrent of sugar and I see the children turning around to look for themselves then turning to pillars of salt and the lightning flash freezes and and and pauses in the space between cymbal thunderclaps and bam! They are lying down on therapeutic chaises their selves illuminated illuminating themselves illuminating the light gone clear and the noises silenced then the lightning flashes pastel pink baby blue again and the drums roll again and the rave the circus the bacchanal the tornado begins again human animals ripping through words covered in a delicious whipped marshmallow meringue frosting.

MAENAD 1. What if nothing is coming? What if I'm in the wrong place?

MAENAD 2. Stay nowhere. See what happens.

MAENAD 3. There can never be a nowhere.

MAENAD 1. Did you know the sun can't penetrate clouds? The salt is too small and dense to let light in.

The sun hits the clouds and immediately bounces back as reflection.

MAENAD 2. So, nothing can be generated or perish completely?

MAENAD 1. As the droplets expand and disperse, light scatters throughout the cloud, creating a blue or green hue. You can predict the weather based on those color changes. But it's not like the white disappeared. The circumstances merely shifted.

MAENAD 3. [*showing with hands*] The Universe is broad at the top, narrow at the middle, and once again broad at the bottom. Like an hourglass. Isn't that ironic? It really is the shape of time.

MAENAD 1. Hm, so if there is a center and an edge, then there can be a void. But, I thought void was impossible.

MAENAD 2. You know, God could be in those gaps.

All pause, ***burst*** *out laughing.*

MAENAD 3. The sky is constantly playing tricks on us. We think we know what we are seeing, but we don't. It's just that the sun is so incredibly red that no other color can be seen at that time.

MAENAD 1. So, are you saying the sun rules our eyesight for a few minutes every day?

MAENAD 2. And the clouds are constantly absorbing those wavelengths?

MAENAD 3. Exactly. The universe is transformed and multiplied into everything else. There will always be an infinite number of universes to be followed by another infinite number of universes.

MAENAD 1. Man, you have to believe in an abundant universe; otherwise, we should all just give up now. These periods of nothingness are continually replenished then used up again.

MAENAD 2. I feel light.

MAENAD 3. I can wander and expand.

MAENAD 1. I can be the sharp acidic taste on your tongue.

MAENAD 2. Is it hot in here? Is it hot in here? Is it hot in here? I'm burning up. Feel my forehead.

MAENAD 3 puts her palm to MAENAD 2's head.

MAENAD 2. No, not your palm! The back of your hand, you idiot!

MAENAD 3. Why?

MAENAD 2. Didn't your mother ever teach you that? Something about your palms being too hot to tell the difference between a warm door and a burning home.

MAENAD 3. Jeez, sorry.

Turns palm.

MAENAD 2. Feel my hands, they're all clammy. I feel

dizzy, I feel like there is a bonfire in my insides. Am I glowing? I'm glowing, aren't I? I think I took too much.

MAENAD 3. You're crazy, I feel amazing.

MAENAD 2. Does anyone have any water? I'm insatiably thirsty.

MAENAD 3. Over an hour ago, I felt this incredible pressure on my brain, as though it was compressing and expanding simultaneously. Life feels pretty endless right now, you know? I feel fucking immortal. In my lifelessness I feel full of nothing but life. My mind has separated from my body. I am completely solid. Float away! See you! Bye bye!

Hysterical laughter, arms wrapped around belly, as though the laughs will leap out otherwise. And, maybe, they do.

MAENAD 2. Is this the end? Is this how I die? After death, memories will be my ghost. In that case, was I ever memorable before the moment of death?

MAENAD 3. Don't be so dramatic.

MAENAD 1. The universe is unchanging, uniform, perfect, necessary, timeless. There are no flaws. One couldn't exist without the other: matter without motion is antimatter, motion without matter is antimotion.

MAENAD 3. I think they call that inertia.

Silence, as though they've heard that word before.

MAENAD 3. Imagine walking on the ocean floor—the smooth softness giving slightly as you walk weightlessly, slightly bouncing, hands outstretched in searching-blindly-pose. You are constantly resisting floating upwards, resisting reaching air, and holding your breath for as long as it takes.

All three hold their breath and release in a collective sigh.

MAENAD 3. You're pulling yourself down and forward simultaneously.

MAENAD 1. Toward what?

MAENAD 2. Or who?

MAENAD 3. Just imagine it as a wrestling match.

MAENADS 2+3 begin to move in a circle facing one another half bent over arms at the ready, a bit of a tango.

MAENAD 3. A slow push toward one another. Imagine fighting the weight of the ocean until you're fighting each other. Your feet cushioned. Eventually you reach one another, and as you push each other's chests away with two open palms, you both fall backwards for a lifetime, hands and legs flailing, expecting to crash through the center from all that weight and pressure, but, instead, you hit silently and sink microscopically.

MAENAD 1. There is give at the bottom of the ocean.

MAENAD 2. Look up.

All turn eyes and heads and necks crane upward as far as they can go. Considering they are already laying down on their backs, they might have to do backbends.

> MAENAD 2. Those ocean ripples are the clouds in your sky. Those flares are your millions of suns. If you're lucky, you will reach the surface and immediately dry to pumice from the impact of the heat and dust particles. This is your raft, your escape, your alien ship ride home. Or, your funeral pyre, depending on how you look at it.

Strobe light. Music begins to pump pump smoke in colors human eyes can't even imagine. The strobe lights intensify, drawing out the scene, the audience begins to hallucinate.

Darkness.

Lights up. HONEY and the YOGA INSTRUCTOR, now playing the role of a LION (he should look like Bert Lahr, clearly a man in a lion suit), walk in holding witch hazel divining wands. They test the earth for signs of gemstones, metals, gravestones, and water. They talk away from one another, never making eye contact. HONEY continues to do that thing where she's mostly talking to herself out loud.

The three MAENADS lay stones down for them to walk on, on account of the stage being covered in molten lava.

HONEY. Are you curious?

LION. Of course, but clarity leads to terrifying hallucinations.

HONEY. My ocean has become a small creek and suddenly I can feel my own vastness again.

LION. [*shivering*] Sure, the mysteries baffle me but they baffle me so much I don't attempt to understand them.

HONEY. What is the ocean but a salted river encircling the world? Are open eyes an act of fear?

LION. I had never seen a magical swallowing of the earth like that before. The bridge was enshrouded in pink cloud dust. You and I debated stopping to take a picture but we were both too lazy, so we passed by a once-in-a-lifetime opportunity.

HONEY. We had the beach, at least, and the rocky sand that was like the inside of a fish tank.

LION. You collected driftwood while I suffered, but

really didn't. I was wrapped in my Scottish blanket, thinking of nothing except the diner coffee I would have, or some kind of warmth, some kind of not caring or shallow caring, to save me, us.

HONEY. [*struggling to remember*] There was this smell, a smell somewhere between body and earth and a hint of coffee.

LION. [*as though possessed*] I'm looking for someone with a beautiful mouth, containing nothing but echoes.

HONEY. Echoes? How does sound travel below the earth? Is there reverb in a grave?

LION. No, I think it's like a cotton ball. Absorbing all the sounds. No, the sounds here are vertical.

HONEY. [*dropping her wand and placing her ear to the ground*] It sounds like a sweet happy pain. It reminds me of my body.

LION. The past is an out-of-body experience; the present is in the body. That is why it is so uncomfortable, I think. We're all looking for water, signs of life. We're all following Ley lines, looking for indications, impressions of a person.

HONEY. [*starting to find stones and arranging them*] I am looking for a solitary stone to sit upon, to save my aching feet. I am barefoot in a forest thick with pine needles. My soles bleed. When I look up from tending my wounds, I am surrounded by swarms of snow swallowing me with an ermine tongue.

LION. Your words cut like icicles falling from nearby storm drains.

HONEY. I begin to sink to nowhereness, anchoring my scarred feet to any bottom I can find. My arms upwardly and outwardly spread as wide as the biggest bird's wingspan. Next, [*stacking hands as though they were the stones*] I stack my stones one on top of the other as tall as skyscrapers. Can I see you yet? I hold my hand to shade my eyes, squint as though that would help me see further.

Holds hand to eye and searches the horizon.

HONEY. Hello? Are you there? Can you see me?

LION. [*shouting back with hands cupping mouth*] I am drowning in this distance. The space between us tastes salty and triangular, practically Bermudian. I've seen lengths of waves and measured salt in beakers, tested the strength and tried to make wine. But nothing works. I think it's because I am not made of mud, but of a rubber membrane. So all my inhales filled my skin to a form.

HONEY. Those inhales are drowning me.

LION. And fingerprints leave their mark on my skin like the rings of trees. I bet you could map out my life through the patterns in my flesh.

HONEY. Sometimes your body feels organ-less, like you are a heliumed balloon. Eyes wide cheeks burst face red hands grasping.

LION. A desperate position.

HONEY. You're on another plane.

THERAPIST. Meet me there.

Pause.

HONEY. I think you're missing a crucial element. If we are no longer defined by the direction we're moving in, a gulf will pressurize us into silence.

LION. A gulf is both a way to hold on and a way to push off. The sound here is deep and wide and formed by floods of memory carving the structures and receding away. I think I can swim across my scream to your echo, the reverb protected by this anchorage.

They pause. They finally look at one another in silence. They lean in to smell something, testing each other's faces with their noses. HONEY takes her divining wand and sticks it down the LION's throat. His eyes widen. Blood rises and fills the opaqueness of his eyes. His copper mane turns to straw. He roars silently, mouth agape. Is air going in or out? Or not at all? He collapses on a stone, aura withering.

Shouts and ravings of lunatics.

Three hooded figures, probably our MAENADS, enter from the wings. They bend down to lift the LION above their heads and walk offstage to deafening drumming and brass. They whoop, hoot, and holler. HONEY has been so still this whole time. Arms limp at her side. Oh what has she done? She doesn't even know. Abruptly, she continues to dowse the ground, slowly walking offstage, following the movement of the dirge.

Curtains draw.

ACT II

Lights up.

We see the MAENADS and HONEY lying naked on a jade floor in a spa. They can have small terry cloth towels draped over their sweating bodies, if they're feeling modest. There are other bodies walking around naked and the MAENADS are at once completely noticed and completely unnoticed from all the forced unnoticing.

It is really, really hot in here. Doesn't it feel good, though? To get all those toxins out? To feel like you're cleansing yourself to the point of passing out? To dip your body in boiling tubs of mugwort tea (it soothes those female problems)? You're probably dehydrated, but who cares! It feels great! All your pores are opening and all this shit is just pouring out of those pores so everyone's faces are blotched red and white and black all over with pus and pimples and scars so later, when you sit with the others eating banchan, you lose your appetite just looking at their faces.

The MAENADS and HONEY are lying down on their stomachs on small quilted blankets and talking, no, gossiping, so the words come out pained and compressed.

MAENAD 1. What happened?

MAENAD 2. Things got a little out of hand.

HONEY. I feel like it didn't even happen. Like we imagined it all.

MAENAD 3. [*rubbing stomach*] If it never happened, we wouldn't all feel this way today.

HONEY. But there are so many parts that are just missing from my memory.

MAENAD 3. [*rubbing MAENAD 2's stomach*] Honey,

you were practically rabid.

MAENAD 1. [*playfully vicious*] Man-eater.

MAENAD 3. Person-eater.

HONEY. [*confused*] What did I do?

MAENAD 2. [*rubbing MAENAD 1's stomach*] You don't remember?

MAENAD 3. You were ravenous.

MAENAD 1. Violent.

HONEY. I remember tearing off costumes, flinging feathers and fur and beads and sequins into the night. I remember the goat roasting. I remember being naked, glowing, jellyfish innards, vulnerable, yet impenetrable.

MAENAD 2. We were all naked as Eden, but never further from one another.

HONEY. I'm tired of this. Let's play a little game.

MAENAD 1. Oh goody!

MAENAD 2. I'm in!

MAENAD 3. Me too!

MAENAD 1. Me too!

HONEY. OK, everyone join hands in a circle shape.

Everyone joins hands in a circle shape.

HONEY. Now, I'm going to say a line and the person to my left will say whatever comes to mind, fast though, no overthinking. We'll go around in a circle and gain momentum like a whirlpool. Got it?

MAENADS. Got it.

HONEY. OK, here we go: "Take aim pull your arrow back tautly. Release into the bull's eye."

MAENAD 1. You really nailed it. You really nailed it down. You really hit the nail on the head.

MAENAD 2. The center is the target. The center of the bull's eye. The bull at the center of the labyrinthine bull's eye.

MAENAD 3. Beast of burden blinded by a ceramic arrowhead.

HONEY. Archer's target. Prophet bull. Blinded bull.

MAENAD 1. Bull's eye. Concentric circles whirlpool eye. Sucking-you-under eye. Under and into eye. Aim at the center, let it fly.

MAENAD 2. Seeing red seeing nothing bull.

MAENAD 3. Red like blood reaching air red like wine red sea red like the matador's cloth.

HONEY. Red like an arrow shot blood shot eye bull's eye. Beef eye. Trompe-l'œil fool's eye.

MAENAD 1. Ceramic arrow china cup filled with blood red bull's eye bull in a china cup bull.

MAENAD 2. Diving through the spatter through the ceramic arrow divining arrow.

Moving into staccato chanting. This should be a swirling whirlpool, no, tornado of sensory experience. They are conjuring something. I want to see something rise cyclone-style from the floor and maybe they all go a little mad and maybe their eyes all yellow or roll in the back of their heads, or something, and maybe their hair all turns to snakes and their voices get that weird deep intonation just like Regan in The Exorcist. And then an elevator door should open somewhere and all the blood in the world should gush out and onto the audience.

MAENAD 3. Prophet bull.

HONEY. Blinded bull's eye bull.

MAENAD 1. Red like anger like the color of the belly like molten metal smith chambers.

MAENAD 2. Prophet bull and sacrificial cow.

MAENAD 3. Telepathic thought sent through flown arrows sent through centered bull's eye.

HONEY. Bull's eye blinded inner world sent extrasensory sensing red. Bull's eye.

MAENAD 1. Lucky bull.

MAENAD 2. Sacrificial eye bull's eye.

MAENAD 3. Now hear voices shut blind through bull's eye seeing red red like oxygen red like wine at the bottom of a china cup red like a feverish bull.

HONEY. Transfer thoughts through hands placed on bull's head send sparks through fingertips communicate with the mute gods.

MAENAD 1. Language less blind prophet bull.

MAENAD 2. Ceramic china cup vessel containing blood bull divining wand divining arrow prophet bull.

MAENAD 3. Crescent moon leaping.

HONEY. Embalmed alive behind blinded eye bull's eye bull.

MAENAD 1. Prophet bull grazing on the ruins of cities.

MAENAD 2. Red like mother bull.

MAENAD 3. Bull blood gushing through shot bull's eye eyeball received on the tongue of the archer. Eternal spectral bull. Blood bath bloodshot eyeball bull's eye arrowshot.

HONEY. Raging bull at the center of the concentric circle labyrinthine bull's eye shot through the bull's eye with bull's horn arrow stretched taut released into the blindness in defiance of the gods' bull.

This whole time they haven't taken a breath. This has all been one giant inhale. Their faces are all red from lack of oxygen. The breaths release themselves in hysterical laughter. The laughter goes on and on.

They lie their heads
on top
of each other's
laps, Lincoln Logs style.
Vibrations make them
laugh even
harder and longer.

Beat.

HONEY. [*getting it together*] Now the same thing but in a line shape.

The four line up lying down, backs of their heads on bellies, legs splayed, in a line shape.

HONEY. There have been reports that the earth is so soft now, people sink and slip through the other side, appearing covered in goo like they had just gone through a water park ride through the earth's intestinal tract.

MAENAD 1. Soft sunken people ride through the earth's bowels.

MAENAD 2. Sunken bowel, softening people.

MAENAD 3. Soft, people bow.

HONEY. Bow.

All sit up and bow.

HONEY. They are so well lubricated they can luge around the edges of the earth straight back home.

Gravity may be long gone but physics is still very much alive.

MAENAD 1. The edges of the earth are home. There is no gravity in alive.

MAENAD 2. Gravity is not alive on the edges of the earth.

MAENAD 3. The edge of gravity.

HONEY. Grave edges.

All lie down on one another, heads resting on chests, arms crossed, eyes closed.

HONEY. Welcomed home, the travelers return to their lives as though nothing had happened. And it is such a common occurrence, nothing did happen.

MAENAD 1. Nothing happens at the return to a common home.

MAENAD 2. Nothing returns home.

MAENAD 3. Return home.

HONEY. Turn.

All turn on their stomachs.

HONEY. Slippery days slipping by. The new texture of the earth makes walking laborious. We are all more fit for it, at least.

MAENAD 1. Slippery earth, adds texture to our

walks. We fit least.

MAENAD 2. Slippery walks on the least of the earth.

MAENAD 3. The least slippery earth.

HONEY. Slip the least.

All turn on their backs.

HONEY. There is no consequence, no evidence, of our steps anymore, the earth merely bounces back.

MAENAD 1. Any consequences of our steps bounce back on the earth, evidently.

MAENAD 2. Consequences bounce back.

MAENAD 3. Bounce back.

HONEY. Bounce.

All sit up and sit knees to chest with backs facing the audience. Then stand together and exit, two to the left, two to the right.

Curtains. Clapping.

HONEY and the woman who played the THERAPIST, now playing VAMPIRA, sit at a round kitchen table eating bowls of cereal, preferably Kix®. Their white pajamas are also the table cloth, their heads and arms poking through holes. They keep eating as they talk, filling their mouths more and more with the cereal. Their mouths get so fucking full, you guys, I can't understand a word they are saying.

VAMPIRA. What's wrong? You're quiet.

HONEY. [*looking into her cereal, still doing that talking-to-herself thing*] I'm eating.

VAMPIRA. You sure? You seem quiet for a reason.

HONEY. I'm tired. I'm hungover. I'm still full from dinner last night.

VAMPIRA. Okay, well, I enjoyed last night. Did you?

HONEY. Yes.

VAMPIRA. That isn't very convincing.

HONEY. Look, I feel this heavy weight on me. I'm terrified of everything. All these ghosts of future this and future that and futures I'll never be able to see haunt me and pin me down, sleeping on my chest at night sending nightmares into my mind.

VAMPIRA. Am I that evil?

HONEY. My path has shifted entirely since meeting you. I'm here, at a standstill. The horizon is bloodied and closing in on me.

VAMPIRA. You can't conflate love with hell. That's way too cliché.

HONEY. I'm afraid yet I can't stop wanting more. You're my ambush, and I know you are there around the corner, yet I can't stop moving toward you.

VAMPIRA. Fine, you can stay in your bland white chaste heaven with your sweetheart. I'd rather be in hell. I'm the one you'll come running back to when you're suffocated by his expectations.

HONEY. You can pour your heart out but then all you have left is a black hole void, a yawning abyss that burns and boils below like a volcano.

VAMPIRA. You're self-sacrificing. You're committing existential suicide.

HONEY. Sleeping with you is like going to the grave.

VAMPIRA. Trust me, trying to sterilize yourself only increases your thirst and dries your skin, sucking all the moisture from your flesh, aging you. Sex makes your skin snap. If you can't handle it, then desert yourself, remove yourself from the living, 'cause this is what the living do, Honey.

HONEY. [*splaying arms, being dramatic*] Fine, I'm defeated! Take these futile weapons! God, I long for the days when I still had a little naiveté.

VAMPIRA. Do you think of him when we're fucking?

HONEY. No, I imagine a lush blueberry field filled with the fattest berries, the field stretching for miles.

It's the largest blueberry field I've ever seen. And for some reason the bushes have large ominous thorns and brambles and thick branches winding around and through and between one another. They are a deep forest green and the leaves are thick. The field surpasses the horizon line, the sky mauve and then blood red with undertones of steel. Storm clouds indicate a storm that will never come, giving the sky ulcers and acid in the belly. And the juice, the juice of the berries bursts out of the delicate flesh and runs drips oozes down our chins and we're drunk on the sugar and our skin is stained our lips our tongues our cheeks are stained and gorged and now we're bursting at the seams, too.

VAMPIRA. You're so weird.

HONEY. Would it make you feel better if I said "I want you?"

VAMPIRA. It would! I need those What Ifs of the night, those habitual Oh God cries becoming our city's meditation, those sordid affairs, luxurious miracles surging on the rooftops.

HONEY. Remember that night we sang that song. What's it called?

VAMPIRA. The night's prayer.

HONEY. I watched you oscillate on Molly that night, between all your frail vertebrae, your proud eyes drawn in your lemon way.

VAMPIRA. I watched your veal-like hamstrings.

HONEY. That was the day my indifferent heart was

forced into the profound darkness that comes when chaos spins you and assembles you into a ravenous beast. After that, I no longer had a choice.

VAMPIRA. I'm poisoned by your coolness. My soul trembles and yours shivers.

Beat.

The two women begin to sing together in complete harmony.

BOTH. Good night good night far flies the light but still got love shall shine above making all bright good night good night.

VAMPIRA. Did you say "got love?"

HONEY. Yah, "got love."

VAMPIRA. [*laughing*] It's "GOD's love."

HONEY. Whatever, I like "Got love" better.

VAMPIRA. I always thought it was "firefly's light." "Good night good night firefly's light."

HONEY. I like that better, too.

Beat. Blinks.

Lights out.

Lights up.

We are now in a room full of shining jewels. The light bounces and dances and mingles with the sound of recorded simulations of rain and soft piano in minor keys. I think you would call this a flashback. This radiant world mocks us, doesn't it?

Each stone is organized by color with small folded labels explaining the stone's purpose. Shades of red, blue, green, yellow, orange are on the east side of the room; gold and silver are on the west; black and white are to the north. A large woman with even larger hair, played by a MAENAD in disguise, sits behind the counter giving incense advice to HONEY, who is disguised as a mannequin. Her skin is flooded with blood, the color of amber.

The smell of incense in this room is so thick it satiates our hunger and fills our nostrils so that we become strong as cedar.

(*Deep sigh.*)

The large woman, our MYSTIC MAENAD, leans over the counter with a smoking piece of incense.

> MYSTIC MAENAD. This is a cleansing incense. It's good for clearing out spaces. You want to be careful with onyx, though, 'cause, you know, you're a Capricorn.

In the vague dreamy air, the other two MAENADS have entered the space. They try on poses in the mirror. Arms, legs, thighs, waists shine like oil, undulating like swans passing, all the while surveilling HONEY.

The MYSTIC MAENAD releases a flamboyant sigh, a basin deep and fillable but empty.

MYSTIC MAENAD. Hold on, let me help these customers.

Waddles to the mirror and addresses her co-conspirators.

MYSTIC MAENAD. [*Loudly and dramatically so HONEY can hear*] Your heads, your gestures, your entire auras, sweethearts, are beautiful, beautiful like a beautiful... landscape. Perhaps, though, you've been a bit heavy-handed with the perfume? Eh?

Aside to the two MAENADS.

MYSTIC MAENAD. You smell like poets. And your dresses, those rainbow colors make me panic. [*loudly again*] Here, I would suggest white Amazonite, it'll help with all that inner turmoil.

MAENAD 1. Ugh yes, so much inner turmoil.

MAENAD 2. So much toiling, troubling.

MAENAD 1. Double troubling.

MAENAD 2. Say, do you have any fenny snake?

MYSTIC MAENAD. Shhhh! Quiet you harpies, she'll find us out.

Turns to HONEY and flashes a Cheshire Cat grin, her teeth so white they blind the audience for a second.

The MAENADS feign interest but continue to slyly wreak havoc on the space, picking up stones and dropping them, rubbing them and getting their filthy hands all over the polished stones and crystals and leaving this layer of filth behind them. All the while clearly eavesdropping.

The MYSTIC MAENAD returns to HONEY. She gestures to a small round table in the corner.

MYSTIC MAENAD. Sorry about that. We get a lot of weirdos in here, I'm sure you can imagine. Come, sit, let's get started.

She shuffles cards for an impossibly long time, making small talk, sizing HONEY up. The cards fold in and out of one another, sliding from hand to stack, ruminating. After the deck has meditated, it rests and the MYSTIC lays her palm gently on the top. Eyes closed, she cuts the deck and asks HONEY to choose. The hardest direction. HONEY does not hesitate to point to her stack.

Flip.

MYSTIC MAENAD. The lovers, two heads are better than one, eh?

HONEY. [*aside to audience, or talking to herself*] I hate you and at the same time I love you. I think that's irony.

MYSTIC MAENAD. [*closing eyes, feeling the cards*] I see an image of a floral ballet ripping apart your chest.

HONEY. [*aside to audience, or to herself still?*] I did punish many a flower with 'she loves me she loves me nots.'

MYSTIC MAENAD. You are infused with some venom, sweetheart.

HONEY. [*same as ever*] They caught us laughing but

we stopped ourselves before the shame of our madness sunk in. My face found your chest and anchored there, waiting for the waves of hysteria to pass.

Flip.

MYSTIC MAENAD. 9 of swords—potatoes with eyes, the nightmare card.

HONEY. That word sends chills to my bones. Tell me, do you see rain or mist? I can't tell. When I lived near the sea I had a view of Sweden. There were magpies by the lake, a frozen boat, a bowler hat and an ax, cold sparrows and lighthouses. I was so far north I lived in darkness all the time. Is that the end?

MYSTIC MAENAD. Oh no, that isn't your end. The cards suggest somewhere tropical. Have you thought of the Bahamas?

HONEY. I do do better in the heat...

Flip.

MYSTIC MAENAD. 5 of cups. The card of grief. Have you lost someone close to you recently?

HONEY. No.

MYSTIC MAENAD. Oh. Oh dear. Oh shit.

Flip.

MYSTIC MAENAD. Justice reversed. Dishonesty, imbalance, overly dogmatic. Too moderate emotionally. Sound familiar?

HONEY. I suppose, I couldn't deny my inflexibility in certain matters. I'm afraid of falling asleep
at night
i draw with a pencil
now
pens and open doors intimidate me,
where would i go, anyway?

Flip.

MYSTIC MAENAD. 8 of swords reversed. Liberation. It's time to rebuild that fallen tower. How can you break free?

Flip.

HONEY. Free? I sometimes think I died when I was 10 and the rest has been one of those floating dreams: the kind when you think you're flying but really you're just swimming through thick air. And you're observing yourself, or at least you're observing whatever stayed behind of yourself, from above.

MYSTIC MAENAD. It's a dream about missing legs. It's a real-life thing about loss.

Flip.

The MAENADS begin to fold like paper fortune tellers—
back and forth in and out
moving the frozen tide, exposing a photograph of the moon
(or was it a lamp light?) peeling the blanket of fog over the stage.

INTERLUDE
A HOCUS INTERROGATION

The curtains part on a lightless stage. All that can be seen are the shadows of 10 stones in varying sizes facing each other in front of chairs arranged in a therapy circle. Otherwise, the scene is entirely empty.

HARDNESS. [*babbling*] What happened?

LUSTRE. [*under a breath*] A circle was cast.

PARTING. [*inaudibly*] When did it happen?

DIAPHANEITY. [*stage whisper*] The length of a river ago.

COLOR. [*mumbling*] Equal to the interior of a serpent.

STREAK. [*droning*] How long did it last?

SPECIFIC GRAVITY. [*croaking*] Until the bottom of quicksand.

TENACITY. [*stuttering*] Time: when the hours are marked by bells.

CLEAVAGE. [*hushed*] An instant—or what clocks measure as no time at all.

FRACTURE. [*restrained*] Who or what body part did it?

ALL TOGETHER. [*playing musical chairs*] The men in the horse who carried the weight.

The stones turn to their lefts, shake hands with the stone on their lefts, make deliberate eye contact, then turn to their rights, make deliberate eye contact with the stone on their rights. The curtains slowly close as this is performed over and over and over.

ACT III

ACT III, SCENE I: HONEY'S LAMENT, OR, THE BRIDGE ACROSS THE MOHAWK RIVER (OR, A TRIAL, OR, A FLASH-FORWARD)

Courtroom. HONEY sits alone on the defense side. The prosecution side is filled with piles of puppet body parts. Each pew should have a small pile of legs arms heads, nonhuman and human alike. The jury is also a pile of puppet fragments. The player who played A MAN should play the OFFICER (let's throw him a bone).

OFFICER. All rise.

No one moves because they are all puppet parts.

The three MAENADS walk in from their quarters and sit behind a comically large pulpit. They are wearing the judgmental robes and holding the scales of justice. They bang on the pulpit calling for order for 54 minutes even though no one is making any noise.

Finally.

MAENAD 1. [*nonsense courtroom speak, blathering on*] Ladies and Gentlemen, on behalf of the request of the prosecution, in accordance of the law and forthwill avoidance of public shaming, we the Judges appoint ourselves as the representations of the prosecution. Forthwith all questions and answers will direct from us. In addition, forthwith this trial shalt be a bench trial, in compliance with a hung jury.

Points to HONEY.

MAENAD 2. Ladies and Gentleman, we present you with dead books and antique memories of gravity. This has all rendered mysterious horrors as a siren song to fool the undead.

MAENAD 3. We found her resigned, fumbling and sacrificing, all the effort of her vertebrae scraping against decomposing muscles.

MAENAD 1. [*dramatic neck craning toward HONEY*] And who is representing you?

HONEY. I will represent myself, your honors.

MAENAD 1. Very well. You may give your opening statement.

HONEY. I went out hunting for a lion with a copper face. I left with no metal in my pack, I carried arrows, and a bow, strung with one strand from the thicket of a tragic love.

MAENAD 1. [*bangs her gavel*] Hearsay! Your words swim in lakes of riddles!

HONEY. Crouched low among the grasses, I waited humbly; the sky was so vast I felt compelled to roll my back against the ground and curl tobacco, poison hemlock, under my tongue, sleep, like death, induced.

MAENAD 2. Objection! Leading the witness!

MAENAD 3. [*side lean, side whisper from side of mouth*] There is no witness, you idiot.

HONEY. [*ignoring the interruption*] Like this, I was found, my predestiny forgotten. A blunt edge contacted my brow, burying my head painfully. Twine bound and cut my wrists, my hair balled up in copper fists gave me some pleasure until our yellowed eyes met in recognition.

MAENAD 2. She is trying to fool us with possibilities!

HONEY. [*still ignoring*] Still holding me, he reached for her missing strand of blond, tucked it back into his mane, kissed me and cut my scalp, took one from the conquest and strung my bow with my own hair. Watching this, suspended, I was, miraculously, bloodless.

Suddenly everyone is Capital R Riveted. In fact all the MAENADS have dropped their gavels and now lean in closely, more of that tabular hand-to-chin position.

MAENAD 3. [*dreamily*] Oh, promises uncertain—and they all meant it, they swear, I'm sure. [*suggestively nudges MAENAD 1*]

MAENAD 1. Tell me, what was the strangest moment—the endearing forecast of coming change or your face cast in smoke?

HONEY. Red tears streamed from his eyes, cooling rivers.

MAENAD 2. [*nodding in agreement*] We do indeed live in a red scorched country led by beastly lords.

HONEY. He said, "The future used to be easier." As he pulled my weapon taut I said, "Our fathers tried too hard."

MAENAD 1. I sense vibrations of passion in you, visions of suffering in a good-giving temptation.

HONEY. As his gums were bleeding, a shrill constant buzz filled the plain, the arrowhead placed coolly against my chest. I reached to wipe his bleeding nose —the snap of a pointed weapon against naked flesh hit me like a crow flies but could not pierce my heart. Defeated, he collapsed onto me, and we bled into one another, blood congealing into chaparral and we disintegrated into the grassland until we were a pool of blood and piles of hair, until we were

pretty

little bows

and arrows

until we were two little

and bows and arrows and two little

two little

Staring transfixed at her hands.

MAENAD 1. [*bangs gavel*] Order! Order!

There is still no noise besides her own voice.

MAENAD 1. The jury hath decided to forgo all rebuttal arguments from the defendant side and move straight to the verdict.

Removes herself from the pulpit and climbs down a 10-foot ladder to the courtroom floor. She paces with her hands clasped behind her back. The other ones: calm faces.

MAENAD 1. Ladies and Gentlemen, hear me out. Here we have a tale of a cloistered anchoress forced to live in a tidy room where the air is dangerous where death exhaled final breaths.

Another MAENAD JUDGE tag teams her with a low-five, continuing this emotional speech.

MAENAD 2. It's a tale of a spellbound war-worn woman rendering a liturgy of hours from enclosures, walls, bell towers.

Third MAENAD low-five tag team. Boxing bell.

MAENAD 3. A woman! A woman who spent her days between a grey brick wall and metal gate, pacing the halls and rubbing beads between her nervous fingers.

MAENAD 1 finishes her off.

MAENAD 1. She fell prey to a diabolical look of a vindictive man, unlucky in love. Are we not all complicit in the immensity of desire?

Pauses, looks around the circumference of the courtroom.

MAENAD 1. Therefore, we are all guilty!

HONEY moans and swoons. Close-up of the puppets mouthing horror and disbelief.

MAENAD 2. Order! Order! Quiet in the court! We shall now declare the sentencing for this vile act.

The three MAENADS huddle and confer behind hands, covering whispering mouths.

MAENAD WHOMEVER. Ladies and Gentlemen. We have reached our verdict. Heretoforthwithal as deemed by the high court of [*mumbling over the where*] we do decleeeem that all present parties

(*Parties? Where?*)

are sentenced to banishment! Officer take her away!

Utter chaos.

Lights out.

There is nothing here. It is an empty island. It is an A-frame house on Saranac Lake.

It could be smaller than a breadbox.

Anyway, it's boring, so nothing to write home about.

The three MAENADS lie on the shore of the lake, arms behind heads, eyes closed, relaxation pose.

Pavlova clouds roll by.

MAENAD 1. They say she had those Italian eyes, black brown deep and heavy lidded, and a Greek voluptuous, some would say rotund, body. Her kisses languished as joy, hot as the sun, then cold as watermelon, on your cheeks. Spare kisses ornamenting an otherwise frigid love, a mother with Latin eyes.

MAENAD 2. They say she was an opera singer, throwing her windward cries into the gulf without reason, sobbing, and chuckling, at the jerks that would come and go secretively (or so they thought). Her windward cries falling in cascades.

MAENAD 3. They say she was born yellow. She was called a toad. Her skin would later turn to gold. Each night her son would rub lotion on her back, then she would take her hair down methodically from a loose bun with no fewer than 27 hairpins, and step into the hot bath with no fear. As he watched her he thought, the women of this town have reason to be jealous of this goldenrod woman.

MAENAD 1. They spent their summers on Lake Saranac in an A-shaped rental cabin, escaping the thick heat of East Coast summers. They called it their island. Her cousins were more brave, waterskiing and playing chicken off the dock. She stood with the water up to her ankles and shouted from the shore. Her brother called her an earthworm. She always thought of herself as their mirror, though.

MAENAD 2. She scandalized her father. He would watch from the balcony of the cabin, roll his eyes, and down mahogany-colored drinks in two gulps. They were poor but they were proud and they knew how to pretend to have money.

MAENAD 3. She vaguely glimpsed the edge of another heaven. Another life thrown from the seat of a motorcycle under the wheels of a bus. After that, she made herself a martyr, without respite or an ambitious heart. She liked to tell everyone how lucky we were to be alive. If things had been different, she liked to say, we would, perhaps, be half ourselves.

(HONEY'S INNER MONOLOGUE, OR THE NARRATOR, OR BOTH:)

The balances of gold on Justice's scales have the weight of a deluge. Does the ocean hear more than a creek? You be the judge, God dares you.

My spineless desires, my visions of sublime hearts, are a series of archipelagos. Am I the infant of the sun? Because some dark mystery chose me, me between all and the earth. I am here to sing her secret, in unbridled eruptions of laughter mixed with somber pleasure.

MAENAD 1. And so, she walked the summit of her rented island like a sentinel while the others plunged into the depths below. She liked to climb high, higher than she remembered climbing, higher than him or him or him. She was aware of ravens' wings pulsating above her head, thicker and more solid than the feathers of her memory.

MAENAD 2. She walked the summit of that piercing sound, her night's watchtower built from a day's bricks, below her forms shivering in the azure, and there she walked the summit.

MAENAD 3. Her sobs echoed against the rocks, bringing back the night to their island, asking for forgiveness of a body admired by a man who left by knowing the sea.

MAENAD 2. That man, lover and pest, more beautiful than Venus, with blue eyes defeated by blankness, blank eyes that speckled the gloomy wide circles traced by misery. Misery influenced by a young blond met under the veil of the ocean: of an enchanted girl, but no nymph.

MAENAD 1. She died there of her own blasphemous pride, she insulted the rites, and she invited a cult in, she made her beautiful body food for the supreme. In spite of her honor, she ordered the clichéd intoxicants each night with cries and torment. She pushed the heavens to the shorelines. She bent herself down from her height into the water. Now is the time to lament.

(*Wail.*)

Lights slowly crescendo, so bright, audience hallucinates. Remain in light.

(And repeat the whole thing over again.)

Meg Whiteford is a writer and performer.
She and her work have appeared in New York City,
Los Angeles, and Copenhagen, Denmark.

Thank you to Matias Viegener, Mady Schutzman, Charles McNulty, Jon Wagner, Douglas Kearney, Katie Pearl, and Tyler Crumrine for reading my play over and over; to Adriana Lafarga for imagining my words as images; and to the person who asked me, "why not do it all?"